Why Did the Dinosaurs Disappear?

The Great Dinosaur Mystery

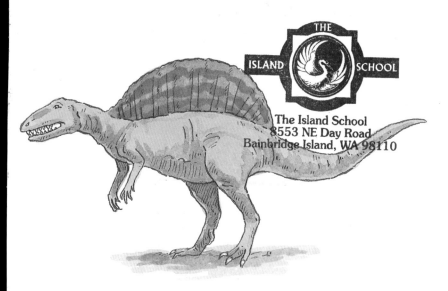

By Melvin and Gilda Berger
Illustrated by Susan Harrison

Ideals Children's Books • Nashville, Tennessee

The authors, artist, and publisher wish to thank the following for their invaluable advice and instruction for this book:

Jane Hyman, B.S., M. Ed. (Reading), M. Ed. (Special Needs), Ed. D. (candidate)

Rose Feinberg, B.S., M. Ed. (Elementary Education), Ed. D. (Reading and Language Arts)

R.L. 2.2 Spache

Published by Ideals Children's Books
An imprint of Hambleton-Hill Publishing, Inc.
Nashville, Tennessee 37218

Printed and bound in Mexico

Library of Congress Cataloging-in-Publication Data
Berger, Melvin.
    Why did the dinosaurs disappear? : the great dinosaur mystery / by Melvin and Gilda Berger ; illustrated by Susan Harrison.
      p.   cm.—(Discovery readers)
    Includes index.
    ISBN 1-57102-033-0 (lib. bdg.)—ISBN 1-57102-026-8 (paper)
    1. Dinosaurs—Juvenile literature. 2. Extinction (Biology)—Juvenile literature. [1. Dinosaurs. 2. Extinction (Biology)] I. Berger, Gilda. II. Harrison, Susan, ill. III. Title. IV. Series.
QE862.D5B487   1995
567.9'1—dc20   94-29806
                            CIP
                            AC

Why Did the Dinosaurs Disappear? is part of the **Discovery Readers**™ series. **Discovery Readers** is a trademark of Hambleton-Hill Publishing, Inc.

Dinosaurs (DY-nuh-sores) lived a long
    time ago.
Then they disappeared.
Animals that disappear are extinct
    (ek-STINGKT).
Extinct means gone forever.
Dinosaurs are extinct.
They will never come back.

3

What happened to the dinosaurs?
This is a mystery.
How do you solve a mystery?
You look for clues.
Clues can help us find out what
    happened to the dinosaurs.

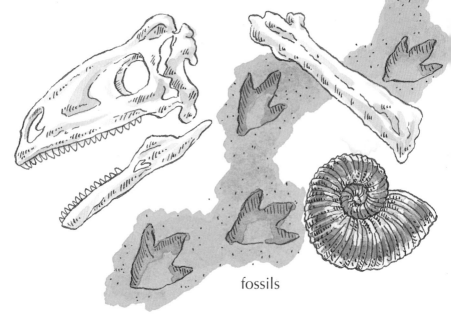

fossils

We get clues from dinosaur fossils.
Fossils are the remains of animals that
    lived long ago.
Bones and teeth can be fossils.
Footprints left in mud can turn to stone
    and become fossils.

We get other clues from rocks in
the earth.
Rocks tell the history of the earth.
The layers of rock are like the pages in
a book.
Each layer contains different kinds of
fossils.
They tell the story of what happened
long ago.

What do fossils and rocks tell us?
They tell us about the Age of
    Dinosaurs.
The Age of Dinosaurs began about
    225 million years ago.
That's when dinosaurs ruled the
    earth.

Fossils and rocks tell us about the
    different kinds of dinosaurs.
They tell us
    —how the dinosaurs lived
    —how big the dinosaurs were
    —what they ate
    —how fast they ran.

Some dinosaurs were very big.
The biggest ever found was
Brachiosaurus (BRAK-ee-uh-
sore-us).
Brachiosaurus was as tall as a four-story
building!
It weighed as much as sixty cars.

Brachiosaurus

9

Some dinosaurs were very small.
One of the smallest was
    Compsognathus (komp-sug-
    NAY-thus).

Compsognathus

Compsognathus was the size of a
   chicken!
It weighed about seven pounds.

Tyrannosaurus rex

Some dinosaurs ate other dinosaurs.
One of the biggest meat-eaters was
Tyrannosaurus rex (ty-RAN-uh-
sore-us reks).
Tyrannosaurus rex was as tall as a
telephone pole.
Its teeth were six inches long!

Some dinosaurs had horns on
their heads.
Triceratops (try-SEHR-uh-tops) had
three horns.
Two of the horns came to sharp points.

Triceratops

Each of these horns was as long as a
yardstick. (That's three feet long!)
The third horn was shorter and less
pointed.

Some dinosaurs were covered with hard,
  bony plates.
Ankylosaurus (an-kile-uh-SORE-us)
  looked like an armored truck.
It was covered with thick plates from
  head to tail.
The end of its tail was like a giant club.

Ankylosaurus

Diplodocus

Some dinosaurs were very long.
Diplodocus (di-PLOH-de-kus) was
one of the longest of all.

From end to end, it was ninety feet long.
That's about as long as a line of
          six cars!

Some dinosaurs ran very fast.
One of the fastest was *Struthiomimus*
  (strooth-ee-uh-MEEM-us).
Struthiomimus could run thirty miles
  an hour!
That's faster than any
  racehorse!

Struthiomimus

millions of years, the dinosaurs lived
all over the earth.
They had no enemies, except for other
dinosaurs.

Then—suddenly—the dinosaurs
disappeared.
What happened to the dinosaurs?

Many scientists have tried to solve this
mystery.
They are called paleontologists
(pay-lee-on-TOL-uh-jists).
Paleontologists study plants and
animals that lived long ago.
They are like detectives.
They find clues in fossils and rocks.
They send many of the fossils and rocks
to museums.

You can be a detective too.
Read the clues.
See what you think happened to the
  dinosaurs.
Then see what the scientists think.

Some clues show this:

During the Age of Dinosaurs, it was
    always warm.
Plants grew everywhere.
The dinosaurs had plenty to eat.
They had lots of baby dinosaurs.

Then the climate changed suddenly.
The earth grew very cold.
It was like winter all the time.

Humans are warm-blooded.
Our body temperature stays about the
    same all the time.
But dinosaurs may have been
    cold-blooded.
That means if the air was cold, they
    were cold.
If the air was warm, they were warm.

Why do you think the dinosaurs disappeared?

This is what some scientists think:

The cold air made the dinosaurs
    very cold.
They could not get warm.
They had no fur.
They had no feathers.
They were too big to hide in caves.
They were too big to build nests.
So they had no way to keep warm.

Also, plants could not grow in
    the cold.
The dinosaurs could not find food.
They could not care for their babies.
Many got sick and died.
Soon all the dinosaurs were gone.

Some clues show this:

A star exploded in the sky.
The explosion sent out powerful rays.
These rays are called cosmic
  (KOZ-mik) rays.

Cosmic rays can hurt living beings.
Animals can get sick and die.

Why do you think the dinosaurs disappeared?

This is what some scientists think:

The cosmic rays hurt the dinosaurs.
Many became sick.
More and more of them died.
Soon all the dinosaurs were gone.

Some clues show this:

An asteroid (AS-tuh-roid) crashed
    to the earth.
Asteroids are giant hunks of rock that
    circle the sun.
This giant asteroid caused a huge blast.
It was like millions of bombs exploding
    at one time.

The blast threw tons of dust and dirt up
    into the air.
The winds blew the dust everywhere.
The blast also started giant fires.
They burned all over the world.
Thick smoke spread from the fires.

Dust and smoke filled the sky.
The dark clouds hid the sun.
The earth was dark all the time.

The clouds were like a blanket.
They blocked the sunlight for many
   months.

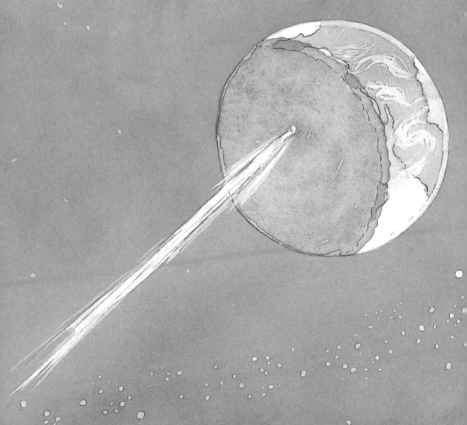

**Why do you think the dinosaurs
   disappeared?**

This is what some scientists think:

Plants cannot grow without
    sunlight.
Some dinosaurs—like *Triceratops*—only
    ate plants.
They could not find any plants to eat.
They starved.
Soon the plant-eaters were all gone.

Some dinosaurs—like *Tyrannosaurus
    rex*—only ate other dinosaurs.
But the plant-eating dinosaurs were
    all gone.
The meat-eaters had nothing to eat.
They starved.
Soon they were all gone too.

So—why did the dinosaurs disappear?

Did they die of cold?
Did cosmic rays kill them?
Did an asteroid end their lives?

No one is sure.

Then in 1992 scientists found a giant
crater.

A crater is a big hole in the ground.

The crater these scientists found is on
the coast of Mexico.
This crater is covered by layers of dirt.
Scientists studied the crater.
They learned that the crater was made
by an asteroid.
The asteroid crashed to the earth from
outer space.

The scientists also learned that the
crater is 65 million years old.
It was formed long before the first
humans appeared.

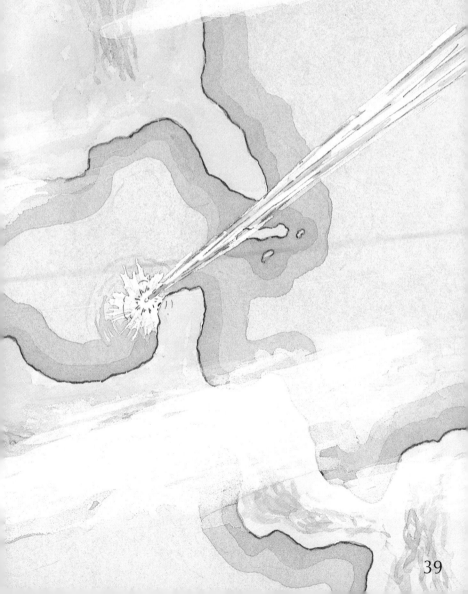

Why did the dinosaurs disappear?

This is what most scientists think:

An asteroid *did* hit the earth.
It *did* raise a giant cloud of dust and
    smoke.
The cloud *did* hide the sun.
It *did* kill the plants.
The dinosaurs *did* starve and die out.

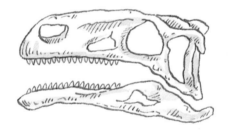

This is one idea about what might have
    happened to the dinosaurs.
It may solve a mystery.
But other dinosaur mysteries remain.

What color were the dinosaurs?
Were they brown or black or green?
Did any of them have spots or stripes?

How long did a dinosaur live?
Did any reach 100 years of age?
What about 200 years or more?

What sounds did dinosaurs make?
Did they roar or squeak or whistle?

Did all dinosaurs hatch from eggs?
Or were any born live?

Every day scientists look for clues to these mysteries.

They go on dinosaur digs.

There they hunt dinosaur fossils.

They look at very old rocks.

They put bones and fossils together to make skeletons and exhibits for museums.

The clues are everywhere.
Maybe you'll find some yourself!

Index